eam Spirit

THE PITTSBURGH STEELERS

BY

MARK STEWART

Content Consultant
Jason Aikens
Collections Curator
The Professional Football Hall of Fame

NORWOOD HOUSE PRESS
CHICAGO, ILLINOIS

Norwood House Press
P.O. Box 316598
Chicago, Illinois 60631

For information regarding Norwood House Press, please visit our website at:
www.norwoodhousepress.com or call 866-565-2900.

PHOTO CREDITS:
All photos courtesy of AP Images—AP/Wide World Photos, Inc. except the following:
National Chickle Company (7 top); Bowman Gum, Inc. (7 bottom);
Topps, Inc. (9, 16, 20, 21, 29, 34 right, 35 top and left,
40 top and bottom & 43); TCMA, Inc. (14);
Exhibit Supply Company (28); Author's collection (34 left).
Special thanks to Topps, Inc.

Editor: Mike Kennedy
Designer: Ron Jaffe
Project Management: Black Book Partners, LLC.
Special thanks to: Jan Paul Matthews and Nancy Volkman.

LIBRARY OF CONGRESS CATALOGING-IN-PUBLICATION DATA

Stewart, Mark, 1960-
   The Pittsburgh Steelers / by Mark Stewart ; with content consultant Jason
Aikens.
       p. cm. -- (Team spirit)
   Summary: "Presents the history, accomplishments and key personalities of
the Pittsburgh Steelers football team. Includes timelines, quotes, maps,
glossary and websites"--Provided by publisher.
   Includes bibliographical references and index.
   ISBN-13: 978-1-59953-063-5 (library edition : alk. paper)
   ISBN-10: 1-59953-063-5 (library edition : alk. paper)
   1. Pittsburgh Steelers (Football team)--History--Juvenile literature. I.
Aikens, Jason. II. Title. III. Series: Stewart, Mark, 1960- Team spirit.
   GV956.P57S85 2007
   796.332'640974886--dc22
                                            2006015308

COVER PHOTO: Jeff Hartings, Ben Roethlisberger, and Alan Faneca celebrate a
Pittsburgh touchdown during Super Bowl XL.

Table of Contents

SPORTS WORDS & VOCABULARY WORDS: In this book, you will find many words that are new to you. You may also see familiar words used in new ways. The glossary on page 46 gives the meanings of football words, as well as "everyday" words that have special football meanings. These words appear in **bold type** throughout the book. The glossary on page 47 gives the meanings of vocabulary words that are not related to football. They appear in ***bold italic type*** throughout the book.

Meet the Steelers

Winning a football game demands good teamwork and great **team chemistry**. It took the Pittsburgh Steelers many years to learn this lesson, and they have never forgotten it. To this day, their goal each Sunday is to hit a little harder, think a little faster, and always be ready to make a game-winning play.

When you pull on a black, gold, and white Steelers jersey, you know this is what will be expected of you. Whether you are a star or a **substitute**, you must memorize the **playbook** and know more about your opponent than he knows about himself. On game days, the players know that they represent an entire hard-working city.

The Steelers have been one of the most clever and confident teams in sports for more than 30 years. They play hard and play smart. More importantly, they play great team football. As Pittsburgh fans know, you can never count their Steelers out.

Dewayne Washington and Brent Alexander
let the Pittsburgh fans know they are number one.

5

Way Back When

During the summer of 1933, a young Pittsburgh sports-lover named Art Rooney bought a team in the **National Football League (NFL)** for $2,500. He named them the Pirates, after the city's popular baseball club. Rooney had some good players on his team during the 1930s, including Johnny "Blood" McNally, Cap Oehler, Ray Tesser, Armand Niccolai, and Byron "Whizzer" White. In 1940, Rooney changed the name of the team to the Steelers, in honor of Pittsburgh's steel *industry*. Not until 1942, however, did they have their first winning season.

The star of the 1942 team was a **rookie** named Bill Dudley. He was small and slow, and threw the ball with a weird sidearm motion. Still, he always found a way to win. Pittsburgh fans loved him. Just when it looked as if the Steelers were ready to **contend** for the championship, Dudley and their other

Art Rooney and NFL commissioner Bert Bell talk business in front of a picture of the 1933 team.

stars were called away to fight in World War II. When they returned, the game had changed and the Steelers were slow to *modernize*. At one point, Pittsburgh went eight years in a row without a winning season. During the 1950s, the Steelers had a strong defense that starred Ernie Stautner, Dale Dodrill, Bill McPeak, Jerry Shipkey, and Jack Butler. But they lacked a great runner and passer. Pittsburgh could have had the two best players of the era—running back Jim Brown and quarterback Johnny Unitas— but the team decided not to **draft** Brown, and cut Unitas during training camp.

The Steelers had good teams in the late 1950s and early 1960s. They were led by quarterback Bobby Layne, running back John Henry Johnson, and receiver Buddy Dial. It was not until the early 1970s, however, that Pittsburgh fans finally got the championship team they *craved*.

Coach Chuck Noll built a *dynasty* around a defense called the "Steel Curtain." It starred linebackers Andy Russell, Jack Ham, and Jack Lambert, defensive back Mel Blount, and defensive linemen L.C. Greenwood and Joe Greene. The team's offense was led by quarterback Terry Bradshaw, running back Franco Harris, an excellent group of **blockers** anchored by Mike Webster, and later two superb **receivers**, John Stallworth and Lynn Swann. This club reached the **Super Bowl** four times in six seasons, and won the big game each time.

The Steelers had many exciting players in the 1980s and 1990s, including Louis Lipps, Rod Woodson, Neil O'Donnell, Levon Kirkland, Kevin Greene, and Barry Foster. They even reached the Super Bowl once more. However, the Steelers were unable to put a championship team back on the field. Some fans worried that they might never win another Super Bowl. To do so, the Steelers would need to find a way to recapture that special spirit and chemistry they had all those years before.

LEFT: Terry Bradshaw stands over center Mike Webster and calls out signals before a play.   **ABOVE**: Louis Lipps

The Team Today

The Steelers spent many years building a roster of good, **team-oriented** players. All they needed was a leader to step forward, a player who could get them to think of themselves as champions. That player turned out to be a good-natured 22-year-old quarterback named Ben Roethlisberger.

When starter Tommy Maddox was injured in the second game of the 2004 season, coach Bill Cowher decided to take a chance and put "Big Ben" in the game. The Steelers lost that day, but they won the rest of their games to finish 15–1—their best record ever. The following season, Roethlisberger led them all the way to victory in the Super Bowl!

Of course, it took the whole team to win the championship. The Steelers do not have any famous superstars, so each player knows that he must play his best every game. This blend of different skills and talents makes Pittsburgh a hard team to play. They are tough and they are tricky. And they play their best in close games.

Hines Ward and Ben Roethlisberger rejoice after a touchdown.

Home Turf

The Steelers have always played right in the city of Pittsburgh. For many years, they shared the same ballparks with baseball's Pittsburgh Pirates, including Forbes Field and Three Rivers Stadium.

In 2001, the Steelers finally got a park built for football, Heinz Field. The University of Pittsburgh football team also uses the stadium. It is horseshoe-shaped, with the open end facing lovely Point State Park.

HEINZ FIELD BY THE NUMBERS

- *There are 64,350 seats in the Steelers' stadium.*
- *More than 12,000 tons of steel and 48,000 **cubic yards** of concrete were used to construct the stadium.*
- *The company that painted the stadium used more than 30,000 gallons of paint.*
- *Jerome Bettis became the 14th player to run for more than 10,000 yards during the first game played at Heinz Field.*

Heinz Field has great views of the game, as well as Pittsburgh's skyline and riverfront.

13

Dressed for Success

For 30 seasons, the Steelers' uniform colors were either dark blue or black and gold, with yellow helmets. For a time during the 1950s, player numbers were added to each side of the helmet. In 1962, the team began using a *logo* that was created by a company called U.S. Steel. It is a circle with three diamonds—yellow, orange, and blue—and the word "Steelers."

Owner Art Rooney was not sure if he liked the logo, so he instructed equipment manager Jack Hart to put it only on the right side of the helmets. When the Steelers won nine games and made

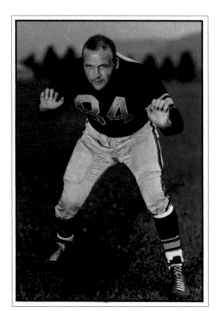

the **playoffs** that year, Rooney celebrated by ordering special black helmets. The logo looked great against the black background!

The Steelers kept the black helmets, and today they are the only team with a logo on just one side. By 1970, the Pittsburgh uniform looked almost exactly the way it does today.

All-Pro lineman Bill McPeak poses in the team's 1950s uniform.

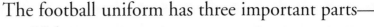

The football uniform has three important parts—

- Helmet
- Jersey
- Pants

Helmets used to be made out of leather, and they did not have facemasks—ouch! Today, helmets are made of super-strong plastic. The uniform top, or jersey, is made of thick fabric. It fits snugly around a player so that tacklers cannot grab it and pull him down. The pants come down just over the knees.

There is a lot more to a football uniform than what you see on the outside. Air can be pumped inside the helmet to give it a snug, padded fit. The jersey covers shoulder pads, and sometimes a rib-protector called a "flak jacket." The pants include pads that protect the hips, thighs, *tailbone*, and knees.

Football teams have two sets of uniforms—one dark and one light. This makes it easier to tell two teams apart on the field. Almost all teams wear their dark uniforms at home, and their light ones on the road.

Jerome Bettis scores a touchdown. The shoulder, knee, and thigh pads are visible on his uniform, as is the team's helmet logo.

15

We Won!

Pittsburgh fans had to wait more than 40 years before the Steelers played for their first championship. Their patience was rewarded with four Super Bowl championships in six seasons. During these years, the Steelers had amazing talent at every position.

Mel Blount

Eight offensive players were singled out for **All-Pro** honors from 1974 through 1979: offensive linemen Jon Kolb, Ray Mansfield, Mike Webster, and Gerry Mullins, receivers Lynn Swann and John Stallworth, running back Franco Harris, and quarterback Terry Bradshaw. The entire defense earned All-Pro votes during this period, including linemen Joe Greene, L.C. Greenwood, Ernie Holmes, and Dwight White, linebackers Jack Ham, Jack Lambert, and Andy Russell, and defensive backs Mel Blount, Glen Edwards, Mike Wagner, and Donnie Shell. Kicker Roy Gerela and punter Bobby Walden were also named as All-Pros. In all, 21 Steelers from this

Joe Greene stretches to block a pass by Fran Tarkenton of the Vikings during Super Bowl IX, while Ernie Holmes (63) and L.C. Greenwood (68) battle Minnesota's blockers.

era were voted the best at their positions! In their first Super Bowl—Super Bowl IX—the Steelers found themselves in a grim defensive battle with the Minnesota Vikings. The difference in the game was Harris, who gained 158 yards against Minnesota's "Purple People Eaters." Pittsburgh won the game 16–6.

One year later, the Steelers were back in the Super Bowl. They faced the Dallas Cowboys, and again the game was very close and exciting. The difference this time was Lynn Swann. He made four beautiful catches two weeks after being hospitalized with a **concussion**. The Steelers won 21–17.

The 1978 Steelers were even better than the first two championship teams. They breezed through the playoffs and found themselves in a Super Bowl rematch with the Cowboys. Bradshaw was the star in a 35–31 victory. He threw two touchdown passes to Stallworth, one to Swann, and another to Rocky Bleier.

Pittsburgh's fourth Super Bowl was supposed to be its easiest. The Los Angeles Rams did not have many stars, but they were very tough on the field. They led the Steelers 19–17 in the fourth quarter. Two long passes from Bradshaw to Stallworth—and an **interception** by Lambert—helped Pittsburgh to win 31–19.

The Steelers and Cowboys met again at the end of the 1995 season in Super Bowl XXX. The Cowboys got their **revenge** with a 27–17 victory. Pittsburgh fans would have to keep waiting for their fifth Super Bowl win. Ten years later, 23-year-old Ben Roethlisberger led the Steelers through the playoffs and into Super Bowl XL against the Seattle Seahawks.

The young, quick Seahawks outplayed the Steelers in the first half, but missed some opportunities to score. That cost them in the second half, when Pittsburgh came alive. Roethlisberger hit Hines Ward with two long passes, and receiver Antwaan Randle-El—who had been a quarterback in college—took a hand-off from Roethlisberger and threw a touchdown pass to Ward that won the game. The final score was 21–10.

Antwaan Randle-El throws a pass to Hines Ward in Super Bowl XL. This play caught the Seattle Seahawks by surprise and won the game for the Steelers.

Go-To Guys

To be a true star in the NFL, you need more than fast feet and a big body. You have to be a "go-to guy"—someone the coach wants on the field at the end of a big game. Steelers fans have had a lot to cheer about over the years, including these great stars…

THE PIONEERS

ERNIE STAUTNER   Defensive End

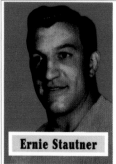

Ernie Stautner

TACKLE-STEELERS

- BORN: 4/20/1925   • DIED: 2/16/2006
- PLAYED FOR TEAM: 1950 TO 1963

Ernie Stautner may have been small for a defensive lineman, but no one in the NFL played more ***aggressively*** or hit harder than he did during the 1950s.

JOE GREENE   Defensive Tackle

- BORN: 9/24/1946   • PLAYED FOR TEAM: 1969 TO 1981

"Mean" Joe Greene was one of the hardest people in history to block. He was in motion the instant the ball was **snapped**, and was one of the strongest men ever to play the game.

TERRY BRADSHAW   Quarterback

- BORN: 9/2/1948 • PLAYED FOR TEAM: 1970 TO 1983

Terry Bradshaw came to the NFL with a lot of talent but very little confidence. Not until the Steelers showed they believed in him did he become one of history's best quarterbacks.

JACK LAMBERT   Linebacker

- BORN: 7/8/1952 • PLAYED FOR TEAM: 1974 TO 1984

Jack Lambert was more than just a great tackler. When he thought an opponent was going to throw the ball, he was quick enough to drop back and intercept a pass.

FRANCO HARRIS   Running Back

- BORN: 3/7/1950 • PLAYED FOR TEAM: 1972 TO 1983

Franco Harris was a big running back who ran like a little one. Despite his great size, he could stop, start, and change direction in the blink of an eye. Harris was voted to the **Pro Bowl** nine years in a row.

LYNN SWANN   Receiver

- BORN: 3/7/1952 • PLAYED FOR TEAM: 1974 TO 1982

Lynn Swann was a fast and *elusive* pass-catcher who had excellent concentration. For many years, he and John Stallworth formed the NFL's best receiving duo.

LEFT: Ernie Stautner   **ABOVE**: Terry Bradshaw

ROD WOODSON   Cornerback

- BORN: 3/10/1965
- PLAYED FOR TEAM: 1987 TO 1996

Rod Woodson's daring style tempted many quarterbacks to challenge him. This was usually a mistake. Woodson came back from a terrible knee injury to help the Steelers reach Super Bowl XXX.

LEVON KIRKLAND   Linebacker

- BORN: 2/17/1969 • PLAYED FOR TEAM: 1992 TO 2000

Few teams tried to run the ball up the middle when Levon Kirkland was on the field. He was strong enough to push blockers out of the way, and quick enough to tackle the fastest running backs.

JEROME BETTIS   Running Back

- BORN: 2/16/1972 • PLAYED FOR TEAM: 1996 TO 2005

Jerome Bettis gained 1,000 or more yards in each of his first six seasons with the Steelers. He was so difficult to stop that he was nicknamed the "Bus."

HINES WARD   Receiver

- BORN: 3/8/1976 • FIRST SEASON WITH TEAM: 1998

Hines Ward became known for "doing it all" with the Steelers—catching, running, throwing, blocking, and tackling. He was voted **Most Valuable Player (MVP)** of Super Bowl XL.

TROY POLAMALU   Safety

- BORN: 4/19/1981
- FIRST SEASON WITH TEAM: 2003

Troy Polamalu became one of the best tacklers in the the NFL when he joined the Steelers. His long hair also made him easy to spot on the field.

BEN ROETHLISBERGER   Quarterback

- BORN: 3/2/1982
- FIRST SEASON WITH TEAM: 2004

Ben Roethlisberger was forced to be the team's regular quarterback two games into his rookie season, and the Steelers won every game he started. In his second season, "Big Ben" led Pittsburgh to the Super Bowl.

On the Sidelines

The heart and soul of the Steelers since their very first season has been the Rooney family. Art Rooney loved football and worked hard to make the game more popular. Dan Rooney continued his father's work after he died in 1988. Dan's son, Art II, later became team president.

The Rooneys believed in the importance of having a strong coach. In the years after World War II, Jock Sutherland turned the Steelers into one of the NFL's best defensive teams. In the late 1950s, Buddy Parker put together a group of experienced players, and the Steelers were one of the better teams in the NFL.

The greatest Pittsburgh coach was Chuck Noll, who won 209 games. He knew what *motivated* each of the Steelers to reach the next level. Rather than giving team **pep talks**, he would talk to players privately. Noll was very cool and showed no emotion.

The team's next coach, Bill Cowher, was just the opposite. He would get so excited talking to his team that players sometimes found themselves showered in spit! Cowher's energy and enthusiasm helped his team win the Super Bowl.

Coach Bill Cowher shares his feelings with an official.

25

One Great Day

When the Steelers met the Indianapolis Colts in the AFC Championship game, everyone knew what was at stake. The winner would get to play the Denver Broncos for a chance to go to the Super Bowl. The loser would go home. Most experts picked the Colts to win. They were playing in front of their own fans, on their own field, the noisy RCA Dome.

The Steelers needed to play a near-perfect game, and they did. They made very few mistakes, and seized the rare opportunities the Colts gave them. With less than two minutes left, Pittsburgh clung to a 21–18 lead.

With the ball on the Colts' 2 yard line, quarterback Ben Roethlisberger called a running play for Jerome Bettis, who was almost unstoppable at moments like this. It was a good plan, but it went very bad.

Bettis took the handoff and tried to crash across the goal line for the touchdown that would finish off the Colts. Indianapolis linebacker Gary Brackett hit the ball with his helmet and it popped out of Bettis' grasp. Safety Nick Harper scooped up the fumble and began racing toward the opposite end zone. Pittsburgh's dream of reaching the Super Bowl had suddenly turned into a nightmare!

Roethlisberger tried to stop Harper, who was one of the quickest men on the Colts. The young quarterback made a desperate dive to trip him up. His hand touched the lower part of Harper's leg and caused him to stumble and then fall, preventing the game-winning touchdown.

The Colts were forced to try a **field goal** to tie the game. They missed, and the Steelers were saved. Bettis, who planned to retire after the season, was the happiest man on the field. He did not want to be remembered as the man who cost his team a trip to the Super Bowl.

"Great play," said a relieved Bettis after the game. "Ben made a great play."

Legend Has It

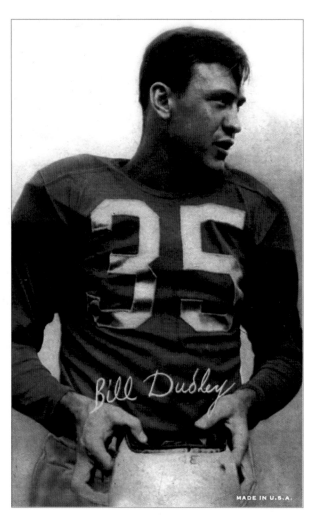

Bill Dudley

Who was the Steelers' greatest "triple threat?"

LEGEND HAS IT that it was Bill Dudley. Kordell Stewart, who was an exciting quarterback, runner, and receiver, may have done those three things well for the team in the 1990s. However, what Dudley did in 1946 has never been matched. That season, he led the NFL with 604 rushing yards, 10 interceptions, and 14.2 yards per punt return.

LEFT: Bill Dudley   **RIGHT**: Jack Lambert

Who had the coolest football shoes on the Steelers?

LEGEND HAS IT that it was L.C. Greenwood. After injuring his ankle early in his career, the defensive lineman was forced to wear **high-tops**. He thought they were ugly, so he painted them gold. This helped stadium announcers tell him apart from teammate Joe Greene when there was a pile-up around the **line of scrimmage**. "Every time I made a tackle, I stuck my feet in the air so the **public address** man could see the shoes," Greenwood once said.

Was Jack Lambert ejected from a game for tackling too hard?

LEGEND HAS IT that he was. In a game against the Cleveland Browns, Lambert was thrown out after a ferocious tackle that left quarterback Brian Sipe seeing stars. There is no rule against hitting a player as hard as you can, but that is what the official accused Lambert of doing when he ordered him to leave the field.

It Really Happened

Pittsburgh fans had a lot to be happy about after the 1972 season. The Steelers won 11 games and were **division champions** for the first time ever. They also made it to the post-season for the first time in 10 years. No one was sure whether they could beat the mighty Oakland Raiders in the first round. But win or lose, it had been an amazing year.

It was about to get more amazing. Late in the fourth quarter, the Steelers were actually winning 6–0. Nothing the Raiders tried seemed to work. Finally, with time running out, Oakland quarterback Ken Stabler tucked the ball under his arm and made a great run through the Pittsburgh defense and crossed the goal line. The Raiders now led 7-6 with less than a minute left. The home fans in Three Rivers Stadium were heartbroken.

After receiving the kickoff, the Steelers tried to move close enough to try a field goal. Terry Bradshaw could not get past his own 40 yard line, however, and there was only time for one last play. Bradshaw dropped back, spotted an open man, John Fuqua, and threw him a **bullet pass**. Jack Tatum of the Raiders moved over to stop the pass.

Franco Harris, the hero of the 1972 playoffs, roots for the Steelers in Super Bowl XL.

Tatum, Fuqua, and Bradshaw's pass came together at the same moment, and the ball *ricocheted* high into the air. Everyone stopped for an instant, thinking the game was over. But rookie Franco Harris kept going. He caught the ball just before it hit the ground and ran 42 yards for the game-winning touchdown!

According to the rules at that time, Harris' touchdown would not have counted had the ball bounced off his teammate, Fuqua. Did Fuqua touch the ball last, or did Tatum? The officials ruled that it was a "clean" catch— the touchdown counted. This play went down in history as the "Immaculate Reception."

Team Spirit

Pittsburgh has some of the most *passionate* fans in the NFL. They are easy to spot in the stands at Heinz Field. Many are wearing construction hard-hats, and some have painted their bodies black, gold, and white. They wave their "Terrible Towels" and sing the Steelers' fight song, to the tune of 'The Pennsylvania Polka."

On game days, thousands of people gather at the homes of friends or at local taverns to watch their team on big TVs. Fans with a major appetite might order a "Roethlis Burger." At one restaurant, this is a combination of ground beef, sausage, scrambled eggs, and provolone cheese. At another, it is a hamburger with bacon, ranch dressing, barbecue sauce, provolone cheese, and cheddar cheese.

LEFT: A Steelers fan shows off his Terrible Towel.
RIGHT: One Roethlis Burger, coming right up!

Timeline

In this timeline, each Super Bowl is listed under the year it was played. Remember that the Super Bowl is held early in the year, and is actually part of the previous season. For example, Super Bowl XL was played on February 4 of 2006, but it was the championship of the 2005 NFL season.

1940
The team changes its name to Steelers.

1960
Bobby Layne becomes the NFL's all-time passing leader.

1933
Art Rooney buys a team from the NFL and names it the Pittsburgh Pirates.

1946
Bill Dudley is named the NFL's Most Valuable Player.

1968
Roy Jefferson leads the NFL with 1,074 receiving yards.

The Pittsburgh Pirates

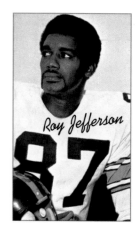

Roy Jefferson

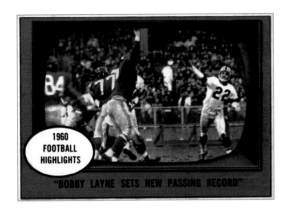

Bobby Layne

Hines Ward

1980
The Steelers win Super Bowl XIV, for their fourth championship.

2002
Hines Ward sets a new team record with 112 catches.

1975
Franco Harris leads the Steelers to victory in Super Bowl IX.

1992
Barry Foster sets a new team record with 1,690 rushing yards.

2006
The Steelers win Super Bowl XL.

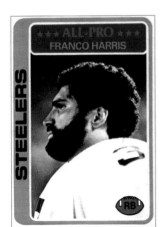

Franco Harris

Bill Cowher raises the team's Super Bowl trophy.

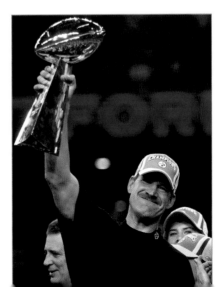

Fun Facts

FACE FACTS

Bobby Layne, who played quarterback for the Steelers from 1958 to 1962, was one of last men in the NFL to play without a facemask.

COMING TO AMERICA

Kicker Gary Anderson, Pittsburgh's all-time leading scorer, dreamed of being a soccer star as a child in South Africa. Anderson's father hated his country's racist *Apartheid* policy so much that he moved the family to America. Until then, Anderson had never even *seen* a football!

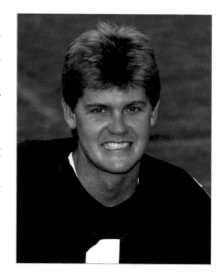

AD MAN

One of the most famous TV commercials of the 1970s was a Coca-Cola ad starring "Mean" Joe Greene. He won a Clio Award for his performance as a nice guy.

A TRUE VETERAN

After playing one season with the Steelers, running back Rocky Bleier was drafted into the army and sent to Viet Nam. He was wounded in both legs, but returned to the NFL and rushed for more than 1,000 yards in 1976.

ARMED AND DANGEROUS

Two of the top receivers on the 2005 Steelers—Hines Ward and Antwaan Randle-El—both played quarterback in college. Quarterback Ben Roethlisberger was a receiver in high school.

SMART GUY

In 1938, Pittsburgh rookie Byron "Whizzer" White led the NFL in rushing yards. He then quit to study at Oxford University in England on a Rhodes Scholarship. During World War II, White became friendly with a Navy officer named John F. Kennedy. Kennedy was elected president of the United States in 1960. He appointed White to the **Supreme Court**.

TOP LEFT: Bobby Layne **BOTTOM LEFT**: Gary Anderson
RIGHT: Supreme Court Justice Byron "Whizzer" White

Talking Football

"I always believed that this town was just as good as any other town when it came to supporting a team. All we had to do was come up with a winner."

—*Art Rooney, on his faith in the city of Pittsburgh*

Ben Roethlisberger

"I could be the worst quarterback out there, but if we come out with a victory that's all that matters to me."

—*Ben Roethlisberger, on personal glory*

"You can go to the bank to borrow money, but you can't go to the bank and borrow a Super Bowl ring. The ring is like a crown."

—*Joe Greene, on what makes the Super Bowl special*

"You should play football for one reason…not to be a winner, not to win championships, not to make more money…but because you love the game."

—Andy Russell, on why he played until age 35

"If I live to be a hundred, I'll never understand how I kept myself in one piece."

—Terry Bradshaw, on surviving for 14 seasons in the NFL

"Guys ask me 'Why are you always smiling?' Are you kidding? I'm in the NFL, that's why!'"

—Hines Ward, on being a football player

Hines Ward

For the Record

The great Steelers teams and players have left their marks on the record books. These are the "best of the best"…

Joe Greene

Terry Bradshaw

STEELERS AWARD WINNERS

WINNER	AWARD	YEAR
Bill Dudley	NFL Most Valuable Player	1946
Jimmy Orr	NFL Rookie of the Year	1958
Franco Harris	NFL Rookie of the Year	1972
Joe Greene	NFL Defensive Player of the Year	1972
Chuck Noll	AFC Coach of the Year	1972
Joe Greene	NFL Defensive Player of the Year	1974
Jack Lambert	Defensive Rookie of the Year	1974
Mel Blount	NFL Defensive Player of the Year	1975
Franco Harris	Super Bowl IX MVP	1975
Lynn Swann	Super Bowl X MVP	1976
Jack Lambert	NFL Defensive Player of the Year	1976
Terry Bradshaw	NFL Most Valuable Player	1978
Terry Bradshaw	Super Bowl XIII MVP	1979
Terry Bradshaw	Super Bowl XIV MVP	1980
Louis Lipps	NFL Rookie of the Year	1984
John Stallworth	Comeback Player of the Year	1984
Chuck Noll	AFC Coach of the Year	1989
Bill Cowher	NFL Coach of the Year	1992
Barry Foster	AFC Offensive Player of the Year	1992
Rod Woodson	NFL Defensive Player of the Year	1993
Jerome Bettis	Comeback Player of the Year	1996
Kendrell Bell	Defensive Rookie of the Year	2001
Tommy Maddox	Comeback Player of the Year	2002
Ben Roethlisberger	NFL Rookie of the Year	2004
Hines Ward	Super Bowl XL MVP	2006

STEELERS ACHIEVEMENTS

ACHIEVEMENT	YEAR
AFC Champions	1974
Super Bowl IX Champions	1974*
AFC Champions	1975
Super Bowl X Champions	1975*
AFC Champions	1978
Super Bowl XIII Champions	1978*
AFC Champions	1979
Super Bowl XIV Champions	1979*
AFC Champions	1995
AFC Champions	2005
Super Bowl XL Champions	2005*

*Super Bowls are played early the following year,
but the game is counted as the championship of this season.*

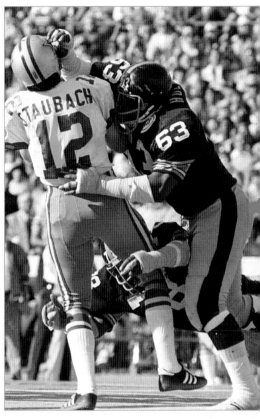

TOP: Ernie Holmes crashes into Roger Staubach of the Cowboys during Super Bowl X.
RIGHT: Chuck Noll and Dan Rooney show the team's first Super Bowl trophy to the fans in Pittsburgh.

Pinpoints

The history of a football team is made up of many smaller stories. These stories take place all over the map—not just in the city a team calls "home." Match the push-pins on these maps to the Team Facts and you will begin to see the story of the Steelers unfold!

TEAM FACTS

1   Pittsburgh, Pennsylvania—*The Steelers have played here since 1933.*

2   Detroit, Michigan—*The Steelers won Super Bowl XL here.*

3   Lima, Ohio—*Ben Roethlisberger was born here.*

4   Fort Dix, New Jersey—*Franco Harris was born here.*

5   Alcoa, Tennessee—*Lynn Swann was born here.*

6   Stockton, Kansas—*Dale Dodrill was born here.*

7   Temple, Texas—*Joe Greene was born here.*

8   Shreveport, Louisiana—*Terry Bradshaw was born here.*

9   Tuscaloosa, Alabama—*John Stallworth was born here.*

10   Prinzig-by-Cham, Germany—
Ernie Stautner was born here.

11   Durbin, South Africa—*Gary Anderson was born here.*

12   Seoul, South Korea—*Hines Ward was born here.*

John Stallworth

Play Ball

Football is a sport played by two teams on a field that is 100 yards long. The game is divided into four 15-minute quarters. Each team must have 11 players on the field at all times. The group that has the ball is called the offense. The group trying to keep the offense from moving the ball forward is called the defense.

A football game is made up of a series of "plays." Each play starts and ends with a referee's signal. A play begins when the center snaps the ball between his legs to the quarterback. The quarterback then gives the ball to a teammate, throws (or "passes") the ball to a teammate, or runs with the ball himself. The job of the defense is to tackle the player with the ball or stop the quarterback's pass. A play ends when the ball (or player holding the ball) is "down." The offense must move the ball forward at least 10 yards every four downs. If it fails to do so, the other team is given the ball. If the offense has not made 10 yards after three downs—and does not want to risk losing the ball—it can kick (or "punt") the ball to make the other team start from its own end of the field.

At each end of a football field is a goal line, which divides the field from the end zone. A team must run or pass the ball over the goal line to score a touchdown, which counts for six points. After scoring a touchdown, a team can try a short kick for one "extra point," or try again to run or pass across the goal line for two points. Teams can score three points from anywhere on the field by kicking the ball between the goal posts. This is called a field goal.

The defense can score two points if it tackles a player while he is in his own end zone. This is called a safety. The defense can also score points by taking the ball away from the offense and crossing the opposite goal line for a touchdown. The team with the most points after 60 minutes is the winner.

Football may seem like a very hard game to understand, but the more you play and watch football, the more "little things" you are likely to notice. The next time you are at a game, look for these plays:

PLAY LIST

BLITZ—A play where the defense sends extra tacklers after the quarterback. If the quarterback sees a blitz coming, he passes the ball quickly. If he does not, he can end up on the bottom of a very big pile!

DRAW—A play where the offense pretends it will pass the ball, and then gives it to a running back. If the offense can "draw" the defense to the quarterback and his receivers, the running back should have lots of room to run.

FLY PATTERN—A play where a team's fastest receiver is told to "fly" past the defensive backs for a long pass. Many long touchdowns are scored on this play.

SQUIB KICK—A play where the ball is kicked a short distance on purpose. A squib kick is used when the team kicking off does not want the other team's fastest player to catch the ball and run with it.

SWEEP—A play where the ball-carrier follows a group of teammates moving sideways to "sweep" the defense out of the way. A good sweep gives the runner a chance to gain a lot of yards before he is tackled or forced out of bounds.

Glossary

ALL-PRO—An honor given to the best players at their position at the end of each season. A "first-team" All-Pro is someone who is voted the best of the best.

BLOCKERS—Players who use their bodies to protect the ball carrier.

BULLET PASS—A pass thrown so hard that it seems to go straight from the quarterback's hand to the receiver.

CONTEND—Play well enough to win.

DIVISION CHAMPIONS—The team that beats everyone else in its group. A division is most often made up of a group of teams that play in the same region.

DRAFT—Select a player during the annual meeting of NFL teams at which the best college players are chosen, or "drafted."

FIELD GOAL—A goal from the field, kicked over the crossbar and between the goal posts. A field goal is worth three points.

HIGH-TOPS—Special cleats that give extra-support to the ankles.

INTERCEPTION—A pass caught by the defensive team.

LINE OF SCRIMMAGE—The imaginary line where each play starts.

MOST VALUABLE PLAYER (MVP)—The award given each year to the best player; also given to the best player in the Super Bowl.

NATIONAL FOOTBALL LEAGUE (NFL)—The league that started in 1920 and still operates today.

PEP TALKS—Short speeches given to raise a player's or team's spirits.

PLAYBOOK—The book that contains diagrams of all of a team's plays.

PLAYOFFS—The games played after the season that determines which teams meet for the championship.

PRO BOWL—The NFL's All-Star Game, played after the Super Bowl.

PUBLIC ADDRESS—An announcement made to fans in a stadium.

RECEIVERS—Players whose job is to catch passes.

ROOKIE—A player in his first year.

SNAPPED—Hiked between the legs. The center snaps the ball into the quarterback's hands to start most plays.

SUBSTITUTE—Someone who fills in for another player.

SUPER BOWL—The championship game of football, played between the winner of the American Football Conference (AFC) and the National Football Conference (NFC).

TEAM CHEMISTRY—The mixing of many talents and personalities.

TEAM-ORIENTED—Always thinking about the team.

OTHER WORDS TO KNOW

AGGRESSIVELY—Done in a way that seems unfriendly.

APARTHEID—A law that once existed in South Africa that discriminated against people of color.

CONCUSSION—An injury to the brain caused by a hard blow.

CRAVED—Wanted very much.

CUBIC YARDS—A measure of a material's volume.

DYNASTY—A line of rulers from the same group or family.

ERA—A period of time in history.

ELUSIVE—Hard to chase.

INDUSTRY—A group of companies that make the same products.

LOGO—A company's official picture or symbol.

MODERNIZE—Change to become more up to date.

MOTIVATED—Inspired someone to action.

PASSIONATE—Having strong emotions.

REVENGE—Something done to get back at, or get even with, someone.

RICOCHETED—Bounced in a surprising way.

SUPREME COURT—The highest court in the United States.

TAILBONE—The bone that protects the base of the spine.

Places to Go

ON THE ROAD

HEINZ FIELD
100 Art Rooney Avenue
Pittsburgh, PA 15212
(412) 432-7800

THE PRO FOOTBALL HALL OF FAME
2121 George Halas Drive NW
Canton, Ohio 44708
(330) 456-8207

ON THE WEB

THE NATIONAL FOOTBALL LEAGUE　　　　　　　　www.nfl.com
  • *Learn more about the National Football League*

THE PITTSBURGH STEELERS　　　　　　　　www.Steelers.com
  • *Learn more about the Pittsburgh Steelers*

THE PRO FOOTBALL HALL OF FAME　　　　　www.profootballhof.com
  • *Learn more about football's greatest players*

ON THE BOOKSHELF

To learn more about the sport of football, look for these books at your library or bookstore:

  • Fleder, Rob–Editor. *The Football Book*. New York, NY.: Sports Illustrated Books, 2005.

  • Kennedy, Mike. *Football*. Danbury, CT.: Franklin Watts, 2003.

  • Savage, Jeff. *Play by Play Football*. Minneapolis, MN.: Lerner Sports, 2004.

Index

PAGE NUMBERS IN **BOLD** REFER TO ILLUSTRATIONS.

The Team

MARK STEWART has written more than 20 books on football, and over 100 sports books for kids. He grew up in New York City during the 1960s rooting for the Giants and Jets, and now takes his two daughters, Mariah and Rachel, to watch them play in their home state of New Jersey. Mark comes from a family of writers. His grandfather was Sunday Editor of *The New York Times* and his mother was Articles Editor of *The Ladies Home Journal* and *McCall's*. Mark has profiled hundreds of athletes over the last 20 years. He has also written several books about New York and New Jersey. Mark is a graduate of Duke University, with a degree in history. He lives with his daughters and wife, Sarah, overlooking Sandy Hook, NJ.

JASON AIKENS is the Collections Curator at the Pro Football Hall of Fame. He is responsible for the preservation of the Pro Football Hall of Fame's collection of artifacts and memorabilia and obtaining new donations of memorabilia from current players and NFL teams. Jason has a Bachelor of Arts in History from Michigan State University and a Masters in History from Western Michigan University where he concentrated on sports history. Jason has been working for the Pro Football Hall of Fame since 1997; before that he was an intern at the College Football Hall of Fame. Jason's family has roots in California and has been following the St. Louis Rams since their days in Los Angeles, California. He lives with his wife Cynthia and recent addition to the team Angelina in Canton, OH.